THE JACOBI & MEYERS GUIDE
TO PERSONAL BANKRUPTCY

THE
JACOBY & MEYERS
LAW OFFICES

GUIDE TO
PERSONAL
BANKRUPTCY

Gail J. Koff, Esquire

An Owl Book

HENRY HOLT AND COMPANY
NEW YORK

Copyright © 1991 by JAMKO Service Corporation
All rights reserved, including the right to reproduce
this book or portions thereof in any form.
Published by Henry Holt and Company, Inc.,
115 West 18th Street, New York, New York 10011.
Published in Canada by Fitzhenry & Whiteside Limited,
195 Allstate Parkway, Markham, Ontario L3R 4T8.

Library of Congress Cataloging-in-Publication Data
Koff, Gail J.
The Jacoby & Meyers guide to personal bankruptcy / Gail J. Koff.—
1st ed.
p.   cm.
"An Owl book."
Includes index.
ISBN 0-8050-1161-7
1. Bankruptcy—United States—Popular works.   I. Jacoby & Meyers
(Firm)   II. Title.   III. Title: Jacoby and Meyers guide to personal
bankruptcy.
KF1524.6.K64   1991
346.73'078—dc20
[347.30678]   90-41495
                                                  CIP

Henry Holt books are available at special discounts
for bulk purchases for sales promotions, premiums,
fund-raising, or educational use. Special editions
or book excerpts can also be created to specification.
For details contact:
Special Sales Director, Henry Holt and Company, Inc.,
115 West 18th Street, New York, New York 10011.

First Edition

Printed in the United States of America
Recognizing the importance of preserving the written word,
Henry Holt and Company, Inc., by policy, prints all of its
first editions on acid-free paper. ∞

1   3   5   7   9   10   8   6   4   2

CONTENTS

ABOUT JACOBY & MEYERS   vii

INTRODUCTION   1

1 / HOW TO AVOID BANKRUPTCY   5   When Debt
Becomes Unmanageable   5   •   Dealing with
Collection Agencies   6   •   Legal Actions   7   •
The Right to Garnishee Wages   9   •   Two Ways to Get
Out of Unmanageable Debt   10   •   Five Most
Commonly Asked Questions   12

2 / BANKRUPTCY: WHO SHOULD FILE AND
WHY   14   A Short History of Bankruptcy Laws   15
•   Who Should File?   17   •   The Down Side   18   •
Five Most Commonly Asked Questions   19

3 / THE PROCESS   21   The Initial Visit   21   •
Exploring the Options   22   •   Bankruptcy
Information Forms   23   •   Appearing in Court   23
•   The Discharge Hearing   24   •   Six Most
Commonly Asked Questions   24

4 / FILING UNDER CHAPTER 7 28 How It Works
29 • Who May File? 30 • Exemptions 31 •
Notification 34 • The Meeting of Creditors 34 •
Discharge 35 • Denial or Revocation 36 •
Effects on Your Future Credit 36 • Five Most
Commonly Asked Questions 37

5 / FILING UNDER CHAPTER 13 39 How It Works
39 • Who May File? 40 • After You File 41 •
Approval of Your Plan 43 • Making It Work 43 •
Discharge 43 • Five Most Commonly Asked
Questions 44

APPENDIX A / CHAPTER 7 BANKRUPTCY
INFORMATION FORM 46

APPENDIX B / CHAPTER 13 BANKRUPTCY
INFORMATION FORM 65

INDEX 85

ABOUT JACOBY & MEYERS

In 1972 a survey conducted by the American Bar Association found that nearly 70 percent of the population of this country did not have adequate access to the legal system. High fees, complicated jargon, and intimidating settings were just some of the obstacles.

The legal firm of Jacoby & Meyers was created with the primary intention of making the law accessible to what is referred to as the middle-income "legal niche." Over the eighteen years Jacoby & Meyers has been in existence, the firm has been a leader in efforts to make quality legal representation available to everyone, regardless of economic and social strata.

In 1977, after the U.S. Supreme Court ruled that lawyers were allowed to advertise, Jacoby & Meyers became the first firm to advertise on television, making it a pioneer in the retailing of personal legal services.

Today Jacoby & Meyers is one of the largest law firms in the country. Composed of 130 firm-owned branch offices in six states (Arizona, California, Connecticut, New Jersey, New York, and Pennsylvania), it has 27 partners and 250 associate attorneys. Each year the firm gives general advice or provides specific legal services to 150,000 new clients in such areas as family law, bankruptcy, criminal law, and personal injury.

One aim of the firm has always been to educate the consumer as to how the law works. This is important for two reasons: so that consumers are able to choose the best possible representation, and also so that they can become the best possible clients for attorneys. To this end, Jacoby & Meyers is pleased to introduce this series of legal guides on specific subjects, such as *The Jacoby & Meyers Guide to Personal Bankruptcy*. In presenting each subject in a clear and readable manner, it is hoped that the legal process itself will be demystified and that the reader will be given a sense of empowerment over his or her life.

Today nearly two-thirds of Americans are in debt; the average monthly balance on bank credit cards is over $1,000 (and many individuals have several). With interest rates on the rise, this means that a growing number of Americans are finding that, no matter how hard they try, they simply cannot keep up with their mounting financial responsibilities.

Whether financial problems are due to the loss of a job, unexpected medical expenses, or an inability to manage credit, declaring bankrupcty can be a confusing and frightening experience. The goal of *The Jacoby & Meyers Guide to Personal Bankruptcy* is to clarify misconceptions about the process and the ramifications of filing for bankruptcy, and to provide step-by-step advice on how to do it knowledgeably without risking your financial future.

INTRODUCTION

Debt is something with which most Americans are all too familiar. Perhaps you've purchased a car on credit. Or you're making monthly mortgage payments on a house. Or, more likely, you have credit card debts that you're obligated to pay off each month.

Whatever form the payments might take, it is apparent that living on credit—some of which is surprisingly easy to obtain—has become a way of life for the majority of Americans.

The figures, which speak for themselves, are rather startling. In 1970 only 54 percent of all American families were in some kind of debt. But by 1983 the number of Americans in debt had risen sharply, to nearly 65 percent. Today, according to figures provided by the Federal Reserve, the outstanding individual consumer debt (and mortgages are not included in this debt computation) averages about $6,500 per household. And, according to the American Bankers Association, users of bank credit cards maintained an average monthly balance of $1,200 in 1988. What's more, only approximately 35 percent of credit card users paid off those balances in full each month, down from the 40 percent that did so in 1987.

How did we get into this fix? The beginnings of the cycle can probably be traced back to the mid- to late 1970s and early 1980s, when high loan interest rates began to appear. Banks and other creditors, realizing that there was money to be made, decided to take advantage of these high consumer loan rates by making it easier to obtain credit. Consequently, standards were lowered, and those who in the past might have had trouble obtaining credit found themselves actively courted by banks and other creditors, such as department stores.

These were the days when you might open your mailbox to find an unsolicited bank credit card just waiting for you to sign the back and use it. The card was nothing short of an engraved invitation to get yourself deeper into debt, and it goes without saying that it took a hardy soul to return it unused.

Unfortunately, many people simply could not handle the growing amount of credit that was placed at their disposal. They used the cards, ran up their debts, and then often found themselves in a quagmire of spiraling charges, as the interest rates on these loans—because that's what they really are—ran anywhere from 14 to 21 percent.

Think about it. If you ran up a debt of $2,000 in one year, at an average interest rate of 19 percent a year, you could conceivably be paying more than $400 in interest charges alone. Is it any wonder that so many people found themselves so deeply in debt that they couldn't possibly see the light at the end of the tunnel?

As a result of this easy access to credit, Americans rapidly ran up the tab. In November 1986 outstanding consumer installment debt—again, *not* including mortgages—stood at an eye-popping $556 billion, which was up an incredible 225 percent from the $171 billion debt that was recorded in 1976.

Of course, the notion of credit itself is not the ogre here. Loans, when they are wisely obtained and carefully thought out, can be a useful and necessary tool of life. Instead, it is poor planning, the lack of a proper budget, or, in many cases, a catastrophic event that makes timely repayment difficult if not impossible.

Obviously there are some people who simply cannot

handle credit. They spend when they don't have, they buy what they don't need, and then they can't pay for it when the time comes. Often it's not even a conscious thing. Debt just seems to add up until it becomes an insurmountable burden.

More often, however, your inability to handle debt may be due to circumstances beyond your control. Perhaps you've lost your job and can't make your monthly payments. Or maybe a devastating illness has struck either you or someone in your family. Or perhaps a family business fails. Or maybe a divorce occurs, thereby lowering your standard of living and making it difficult for you to meet your financial obligations. In these cases, an amount of debt that might once have been reasonable and easily handed suddenly becomes an impossibility.

Then what do you do?

There are, under law, remedies for the predicament. If all else fails, you can declare bankruptcy, which will allow you to discharge some, if not all, of your debts and then start over. Although some might consider bankruptcy a shameful step to take, it is not. Instead, it has become an accepted procedure that can relieve you of persistent creditors and allow you to avoid total financial devastation. Some debtors may even be able to preserve equity in a home or prevent the garnishment of wages (an official notice to an employer to pay part of a debtor's wage directly to the creditor) or other necessary income. In addition, bankruptcy can alleviate the terrible psychological toll brought on by owing vast sums of money that you cannot possibly ever repay.

As we mentioned before, today more Americans than ever find themselves in debt. For this reason, it should come as no surprise that the number of personal bankruptcy petitions—not business—filed in 1985 was 298,045, which represented a *70 percent* jump over the 172,414 petitions that were filed in 1978. But bankruptcy filings reached their peak the next fiscal year, 1986–87, when 561,278 were made, with 84 percent of this figure representing nonbusiness petitions.

Although these figures may not be consoling to those who find themselves in dire financial straits, they should indicate that if you are in a serious financial pinch, you are not alone. And what's more, there is something you can do about it.

In this book we hope to accomplish a number of things. First, we will try to explain how you might be able to handle your debt *without* declaring bankruptcy. If, however, this is not possible, we will explain what bankruptcy is, how it works, how you can make it work for you, and just what kind of personal bankruptcy procedure is the right one for you. (We will not discuss corporate bankruptcy here.)

With bankruptcy, as with many legal procedures, it is desirable to have an attorney who can best represent your interests. Therefore, this book is not meant to be a do-it-yourself kit. Rather, it is meant to provide comprehensive information that will help you decide what's best for you. It should also serve to help demystify the procedures involved in bankruptcy so that you can make an informed decision as to whether this solution is the right one for you.

The idea of filing for bankruptcy can be frightening and anxiety-provoking. However, the truth is that filing for bankruptcy is not as discouraging an ordeal as you may imagine it to be. By showing you, step by step, the procedures involved, we hope to make the ordeal far less daunting. If we accomplish even that much, we will consider this book a success.

1

HOW TO AVOID BANKRUPTCY

When Debt Becomes Unmanageable

Certainly we are all very much aware of those times when we owe money, but what we can't always do is point to the precise moment when this debt becomes unmanageable. For instance, if you make $30,000 a year and your debts, when added up, amount to $3,000, this is a manageable figure. However, if you make $30,000 a year and your debts amount to $15,000, this would almost surely qualify as unmanageable debt. You need help.

The normal rule of thumb is that you are in unmanageable debt when your debt payments reach at least 25 to 30 percent of your yearly net income. But perhaps a better indication that you are in financial trouble is when, after meeting your essential expenses—rent or mortgage payments, telephone, electric, and so on—you can pay only the interest on your debts and are not able to chip away at any part of the principal.

For instance, let's say your credit card debt balance is $5,000 and the minimum payment each month is $300. If you have trouble making this payment, your debt is unmanageable.

Dealing with Collection Agencies

There may come a time when you simply cannot make the payments on a particular debt. Before long, you will receive letters from your creditors requesting immediate payment. After a further time without making payments, you may receive notices from your creditors that demand the entire amount of the debt. If the purchase agreement you signed specifies that on default, or failure to pay, the total unpaid balance becomes due, you are liable to pay this amount immediately.

You may, of course, ignore these dunning letters as they come in. But it won't do you much good. Eventually you will receive letters informing you that your accounts have been handed over to debt collection agencies. These agencies work on a commission basis and, consequently, are not above using collection methods that often cross the line into harassment.

However, if harassment does occur, there is recourse available to you. Legislation passed by Congress controls the practice of debt collection in the following ways:

- Debt collectors are not permitted to appear at your place of business or contact you there in any manner.
- Debt collectors are not permitted to telephone you, ring your doorbell, or contact you in any way at unreasonable or inconvenient times (which would include two o'clock in the morning).
- Debt collectors, when making inquiries about you from relatives, friends, neighbors, or acquaintances, are not permitted to embarrass you by identifying themselves as debt collectors. However, if they don't identify themselves as such, they are free to ask anybody anything about you.
- Debt collectors, whether or not they identify them-

selves as such, are not permitted to question anybody about you more than once.

- Debt collectors are not allowed to violate your
privacy by querying anybody about you by post-
card.
- Debt collectors are not permitted to contact you if
you inform them, preferably in writing, that you
can't or won't pay your debts. Your creditors' only
recourse is to bring legal action against you.

If any of these rules are violated and it can be proved
that you have sustained actual damage because of the
actions of these debt collectors (perhaps the loss of a job),
you are entitled to bring a civil suit against them. You can
also put a stop to further violations of this law by sending
written complaints to the collection agencies, the creditors
who hired them, the local Better Business Bureau, and your
local consumer affairs office.

Another step you can take if you are being harrassed by
collection agencies is to hire an attorney. Once you've done
this, debt collectors are legally required to deal only with
your attorney. They are not permitted to communicate with
you directly.

Your attorney will be familiar with state laws that may
provide you with additional protection against abusive and
unfair debt collection practices. Additionally, he or she will
know how to make these laws work for you.

Your attorney may also be more effective in dealing with
debt collection agencies, which may result in some sort of
satisfactory compromise.

And if all else fails, your attorney will also know when a
civil action against these collection agencies is appropriate.

Legal Actions

If collection agencies fail in their attempts to collect on the
debt, you may expect that your creditors will turn the
matter over to attorneys for legal collection. At this point
you will receive at least one attorney's letter requesting

that you pay the entire amount owed plus interest and costs. At this time, if you can afford to do so, it would be wise to try to come to some kind of compromised settlement in order to prevent a lawsuit.

If you simply ignore the attorney's letters, you will likely be sued. You will receive a summons, which is merely a device to bring you to court to answer a creditor's claim against you. This summons can be delivered by a process server, or it can arrive in the mail.

You may avoid going to court either by paying your debt or by making a reduced-payment deal with the attorney. If such a deal is accepted, make sure you get it in writing.

If you choose to ignore the court summons, a judgment will be entered against you for the amount owed plus costs and interest. A judgment is a formal entry of the court's decision, which states that you are legally required to pay your creditor the sum awarded by the court. Once your creditors have obtained a judgment, they can issue through the court a Bank Account Restraining Notice, which prevents you from drawing against your bank account until you've paid your debt.

Once your creditors have obtained a judgment against you, they (now known as judgment creditors) have the right to examine you under oath to determine what assets you have. This process is known as a *discovery procedure* or as proceedings supplementary to judgment. Once this is accomplished, your creditors may then obtain from the court a Writ of Execution. This document directs the sheriff's office to seize your assets until full payment has been made or until these assets are liquidated (converted into cash), so that the complete amount awarded to the creditors may be paid. Some assets, depending on the state in which you live, are exempted from seizure. The following is a list of some of the major exemptions permitted by most states (the court clerk or an attorney can furnish you with a complete list).

- The house in which you live and the surrounding land, up to a certain limit. However, some states impose a monetary limit: $10,000 in New York; $20,000 if the judgment is against a husband and wife. In California, you can keep $30,000 plus $75,000 in equity, depending on the circumstances.

- Household goods and personal effects including clothing. However, clothing is usually limited to necessities and therefore (in some states) might not include an expensive fur coat or gold tie clasp.
- Personal property up to a fixed amount—$1,000, for instance. This includes bank accounts, money market accounts, stocks, bonds, and other investments.
- The tools and implements of your trade. For instance, if you're a writer, your typewriter or word processor would be exempt. In some states your automobile may be considered a tool of your trade, provided it's necessary for your work—if you're a salesperson, for example—or a tractor, if you're a farmer. In some states motor vehicles are exempt even if they're not tools of the trade.
- Death benefits from your insurance.
- As a general rule, proceeds from your pension plans.

Once full payment is made after your assets are liquidated, you should receive a satisfaction of judgment in the mail. If you do not, contact your creditors and insist that you receive such a document.

The Right to Garnishee Wages

Depending on the state in which you reside, your wages may be garnisheed to satisfy a judgment. In some states you are exempt from garnishment of wages if you're a laborer, mechanic, public employee, or government worker. By federal law, seamen are exempt in all states.

If you're not exempt from wage garnishment, federal law still protects against all your wages being used to repay your debt. The first $48 of your weekly salary is exempt, and total garnishment is limited to 25 percent of your take-home pay. This is the federal law, but your particular state law may be even more liberal.

In some states only one income judgment may be executed at a time. This means that if you have two or more judgments against you, your wages can be garnisheed by only one of your creditors until that judgment is satisfied. Only then can the next creditor in line garnishee your wages.

If there is a garnishment of your wages, federal law protects you from being fired for any one debt. However, if your wages are garnisheed for two or more debts, the law does not protect you. As a practical matter, though, an employer who wants to fire you can always find a legal way to do it.

Two Ways to Get Out of Unmanageable Debt

If you find yourself with unmanageable debts, you can try to use two ways, short of declaring bankruptcy, in order to get out of debt. The first is to take out a consolidation loan; the second is to try to work out a reduced-payment plan with your creditors.

Consolidation Loans

A consolidation loan is a personal loan that is used to pay off all your debts. You can obtain this loan from a bank, credit union, or finance company.

If you are successful in obtaining a consolidation loan, you will, in fact, owe more money than you did before. This is because your debt payments will be spread out over a longer period of time, thus making the total amount of interest you're paying considerably higher.

Yet consolidation loans do offer an advantage: The single monthly payment, spread out over a longer period of time than the previous payments you've had to make, is smaller. Consequently, you're paying less per month, although it will be for a longer time.

As consolidation loans were designed for people who find themselves in serious debt, the mere fact that you owe a lot of money does not automatically disqualify you from getting such a loan. However, today banks and credit unions are giving far fewer consolidation loans. In fact, these days most consolidation loans are granted by finance companies, whose interest rates are higher than those of other lenders. Because the loans are risky, the lenders may also require that the loans be secured by property being put up as collateral, as in car loans, for instance, be guaranteed by one or more credit-worthy persons, and permit wage assignments. You may also be required to carry life insurance (for which you must pay).

Reduced-Payment Plans

The theory behind reduced-payment plans is that by requesting your creditors to lengthen the time in which you must repay your debts, you can cut the size of your monthly payments. The hope is that creditors will be willing to wait longer for their money rather than get no money at all.

If you are considering this option, your first step should be to compile a list of the monthly debts that you have trouble paying. For instance, let's say your monthly debts are:

Credit Card	$75
Department Store	$50
Cash Loan	$75
TOTAL	$200

Next, add up the bills you must pay each month, such as rent or mortgage, food, clothing, medical bills, and so on, and subtract this from your net income. The amount you have left is what's available for monthly debt repayment. Let's say it's $100, which is half of your monthly scheduled payments.

Now compile a proposed schedule of repayments by cutting your monthly scheduled payments in half. This would mean that each month you could afford to pay your credit card company $37.50, the department store $25.00, and your cash loan $37.50.

Your next step would be to contact each creditor and set up an appointment. When you meet with your creditor bring in your list of "must" expenses along with proof of your net income. Show the creditor how much money you have each month to pay your debts and how many debts you are liable for. Make it clear that you are going to use this amount to pay all your creditors equally in accordance with the schedule of repayment you have made. Show the schedule, emphasizing that you are not going to add to your debt and that you will resume full payments as soon as possible.

You must understand that if your creditor does agree to go along with your plan, interest and late charges on the unpaid balance of your debt will continue to mount, making the debt that much larger. But now, if you keep to your plan, your total debt should be manageable.

Just because you come up with what you consider is a workable plan for reduced repayment doesn't mean that your creditor will accept it. The fact is, most will not. Creditors' attorneys seldom recommend accepting a reduced-payment plan unless the debtor makes a substantial initial payment and then agrees to *a confession of judgment,* in which the debtor acknowledges that the creditor holds a judgment against him or her.

Nevertheless, if your debt is unmanageable, it's certainly worth trying to convince your creditors that a reduced-payment plan is in their best interests as well as your own.

Five Most Commonly Asked Questions

1. *How do I know when my debts are unmanageable?*

   If your debts amount to more than 25 percent of your net income, or if you have trouble keeping up with the interest payments on your debts, then you have unmanageable debt.

2. *What will happen if I ignore the letters I've been getting from a local department store dunning me for the money I owe them?*

Eventually the store will probably hand the matter over to a collection agency, which will be more tenacious in its efforts to collect the debt.

3. *Can collection agencies call me all hours of the day and night and harass my family for the money I owe?*

Congress has passed laws in an attempt to control just this kind of harassment. If you sustain any actual damages as a result of the actions of collection agencies, you may file civil suit against them.

4. *I've received an attorney's letter informing me that I am being taken to court for money I owe on a bank credit card. What can happen to me?*

If you can't pay the debt, the company will probably bring a legal action against you to recover the debt plus interest charges and court costs. You will receive a summons. If you ignore this summons, a judgment will be entered against you.

5. *I owe money and a judgment has been made against me. Does my creditor have the right to go to my employer to get the money?*

Depending on the state in which you reside, your creditor might have the right to garnishee your wages. The first $48 is exempt and total garnishment is limited to 25 percent of your take-home pay. Some states offer more liberal protection than others, so it's best to check on the rules of the state in which you reside.

2

BANKRUPTCY:
WHO SHOULD FILE
AND WHY

At Jacoby & Meyers we see thousands of bankruptcy cases each year. We find that the majority of people who file wind up in court for one of two reasons. Either they have amassed enormous medical bills and are inadequately covered by insurance, or they are simply overwhelmed by credit card bills and bank loans. Frequently what pushes them over the edge is the loss of a job.

Despite what some might think, the truth is that most people would prefer *not* to be in bankruptcy court. It is not an especially pleasant experience, and it is certainly not in the great American tradition of "rugged individualism," "free enterprise," and "going it alone." In fact, Los Angeles U.S. Bankruptcy Court Judge Barry Russell maintains that only 5 to 10 percent of debtors filing bankruptcies have filed before (if you have filed within six years, you may not file again). This seems to indicate that the vast majority of Americans availing themselves of the process are not out to defraud anyone, but rather are in need of the kind of economic help the bankruptcy procedure can provide.

If you have unmanageable debt, realize that there is no way you are going to be able to pay it off, under current circumstances are unable to obtain a consolidation loan, and your creditors will not accept a reduced-payment plan, there is another option open to you. Individuals can file for bankruptcy under either Chapter 7 (liquidation) or Chapter 13 (adjustment of an individual's debts), depending on their particular circumstances.

A Short History of Bankruptcy Laws

Our bankruptcy laws have their foundations in eighteenth-century England. As an alternative to spending time in debtors' prison, English law allowed for an individual to declare bankruptcy. To the framers of our Constitution, the idea of spending time in debtors' prison or the alternative of involuntary servitude in payment of debt was loathsome. And so under the Constitution Congress was empowered to "establish uniform laws on the subject of bankruptcies in the United States." As a result, a system of federal bankruptcy courts, with judges appointed to fourteen-year terms, was eventually established. Once this system was in place, debtors had the opportunity to start over again, without the awesome and often paralyzing burden of debt.

Yet it wasn't until the Bankruptcy Act of 1841 that an individual was allowed to declare voluntary bankruptcy. Prior to this, imprisonment for debt was common. In some states prisons held three to five times as many debtors as other criminals.

But, oddly enough, the first bankruptcy laws written in the United States were intended more for the protection of the creditor than the debtor. The purpose of these laws was to make sure that each creditor had an equal opportunity of being paid if the debtor did not have sufficient funds to pay off all his or her debts. Over the years, however, there has been a shift in emphasis; now bankruptcy and collection laws are written with an eye toward offering the debtor the most protection.

Nevertheless, until twenty years ago, because the failure to pay one's debts was looked on as something shameful, those who filed for bankruptcy still felt disgraced. In fact, our bankruptcy laws were even considered a form of punishment, because not only did they relieve people of all of their debts, they also stripped them of all their assets. Thus a fresh beginning was possible, but it meant starting from zero.

The Bankruptcy Reform Act, passed by Congress in 1978, went a long way in helping to change this attitude. In large part, the impetus for this reform came from the seeds sown in 1984 when free credit cards for the average citizen became a reality. Suddenly not only the rich could enjoy ready access to credit. Now everyone had not only the right but the opportunity to go into debt, and many did. The standard of living of the average American jumped, but this did not necessarily mean that his or her income did.

By 1978 hundreds of thousands of Americans found they had run up large debts they could not possibly pay off. Of course there was always the option of turning to existing bankruptcy laws, but these laws were written in such a way that the debtors would be wiped out economically.

With this in mind, Congress passed the Bankruptcy Reform Act. The act expanded the list of items that were exempt from sale when a debtor's assets were liquidated, thus making bankruptcy more palatable to consumers. This act allowed the individual states to either set their own exemption rules or follow those guidelines set by the federal government.

Another facet of the act was that it gave debtors more power to keep creditors away by broadening the rules regarding automatic stays—that is, actions that freeze creditors' attempts to seize assets owned by the person declaring bankruptcy.

The Reform Act of 1978 also addressed itself to the problem of the stigma attached to bankruptcy, in part by changing some of the wording. For instance, the petitioner was to be known as "the debtor" as opposed to the "bankrupt."

The bankruptcy laws were amended once again in 1984. This time Congress removed some of the reforms included in the 1978 act. For instance, a debtor who declares Chapter 13 bankruptcy (which will be discussed in chapter 5) must now apply *all* his or her excess earnings to pay off debts. In addition, rules for other kinds of personal bankruptcy were changed in order to eliminate potential abuses.

Although bankruptcy should never be entered into casually, it is a viable alternative for those whose debts have climbed to unreasonable heights and who see no other way of getting out from under the mountain of bills. For debtors who own a home, bankruptcy may be the only way to preserve equity. It may also be the only way to prevent creditors from garnisheeing wages or other income once the petition is filed.

Who Should File?

People from all walks of life are susceptible to unmanageable debt. Rarely do people make a conscious effort to run up debts and then file bankruptcy, thereby trying to defraud creditors. More often than not, debt sneaks up on us and, before we know it, we are snowed under.

Following are a few examples of the type of people who come through our offices looking to file for bankruptcy.

- A man whose business fails is held personally liable on $75,000 worth of business debts, ruining his previously impeccable credit rating. He finds another job after four months, but he now has numerous lawsuits pending against him. In order to avoid having an income execution, or garnishment, placed on his salary, he files bankruptcy.
- A psychologist is employed by the State of New York, earning $30,000 per year. Her eduction was paid for by taking out $98,000 in student loans. Her monthly payment on these loans takes up almost 75 percent of her net salary and she is falling behind. She cannot file for bankruptcy under Chapter 7, however, because such loans are not dischargable until they are unpaid for five years. But she may file for reorganization under Chapter 13.

- A man makes $32,000 per year and regularly receives expanded lines of credit from major banks—until he finds he is incapable of paying even the interest charges on $30,000 worth of credit card debt. We advise him to file for bankruptcy.

Not one of the people presented in these three examples set out to defraud anyone, yet they all found themselves in an economic bind from which they did not believe they could disentangle themselves short of filing for bankruptcy. Consequently, they came to us looking for help.

The Down Side

Of course, there is a negative side to declaring bankruptcy, and so our advice to potential clients is that they should avoid it if they possibly can. For instance, if your financial problems are only temporary—that is, if you can see yourself getting out from under them some time down the road—then you should certainly refrain from filing bankruptcy.

For one thing, a declaration of bankruptcy is recorded in your credit file and will remain there for ten years. Certainly this will affect your ability to obtain credit in the future. And even after the ten years are over, potential creditors may ask if you have ever filed for bankruptcy. Your response may influence their decision to extend credit. Under most circumstances, you will also have trouble getting a credit card or a personal loan from a bank.

You may still be able to purchase a house, because it is a secured loan. However, it's very probable that you will have to put more money down and pay a higher interest rate.

Obviously, those who come into our offices with bankruptcy on their minds are very concerned about the ramifications. For instance, they worry about being fired from their job if they file bankruptcy. Due to an antidiscrimination law, they cannot.

People also worry about their ability to obtain credit once they file bankruptcy. We remind them that they are really in no worse a situation than before the filing because, if their financial situation was so bad that bankruptcy is justified, they probably couldn't get credit anyway.

But perhaps the number-one concern is the psychological effect. Most people still attach a terrible stigma to filing for bankruptcy. We remind our clients that big corporations, such as A. H. Robins, Paul Revere, Texaco, and LTV, do it all the time.

Nevertheless, you should weigh all these factors before you make your final decision as to whether or not it is in your best interests to file for bankruptcy.

Five Most Commonly Asked Questions

1. *I filed for bankruptcy four years ago, and, once again, I'm in unmanageable debt. Can I file again?*

   No. A period of at least six years must pass before you can file for bankruptcy again.

2. *At what point should I consider filing for bankruptcy?*

   If you have concluded that your debt is unmanageable with little hope of the situation changing, you do not qualify for a consolidation loan, and your creditors refuse to go along with a reduced-payment plan, then it's time to seriously consider bankruptcy.

3. *I owe several thousand dollars on a school loan. Can I file for bankruptcy to avoid paying it?*

   School loans are nondischargeable unless you haven't made the payments for at least five years.

4. *How long can I expect the fact that I filed bankruptcy to affect my credit rating?*

   The fact that you filed bankruptcy is noted on your credit rating for ten years. However, this doesn't necessarily mean that you cannot obtain credit during this time. In reality, after three years of a clean credit rating, you may apply for credit once again and you may well obtain it.

5. *I recently filed for bankruptcy. Does this mean that I won't be able to buy a house or a car for ten years?*

No. It is possible to buy a house or car because these would be secured loans—that is, the property would act as the collateral for the loan. However, you may be asked to make a larger initial down payment and the interest rate may be higher than if you hadn't filed for bankruptcy.

3

THE PROCESS

Once you've made the decision to explore the possibility of filing bankruptcy, your next step should be to visit an attorney. The attorney will examine your individual case, see if you are indeed a likely candidate for filing bankruptcy, and then advise you of your options.

What we intend to do in this chapter is to simulate a first visit to an attorney, so you can get an idea of what to expect, and then take you slowly, step by step, through the process, just as an attorney would.

The Initial Visit

At your initial meeting, your attorney will sit down with you and listen to your problem. Be prepared to discuss your financial situation in specifics. Bring along a detailed list of your debts and assets.

After you've explained the general situation, the attorney will ask you pointed questions about your family income, spending habits, and what your specific debts are.

Then, in order to find out what your assets are (or might be in the near future), the attorney will likely ask you a series of questions that will certainly include:

- Do you own or have an interest in a house, cooperative apartment, or a condominium?
- Do you have any savings?
- Do you own any stocks or bonds?
- Do you stand to inherit anything of value in the near future?
- Are you suing anyone for any reason?
- Have you transferred any property recently?
- Have you made any payments to any creditors within the past ninety days?
- Have you paid any family members or friends within the past year?
- Do you own a car?
- Do you expect to receive a tax refund?
- Do you owe any taxes or money on parking tickets? (These questions are asked because these debts must be repaid.)

Exploring the Options

If, at this point, the attorney agrees that you are so deeply in debt that bankruptcy is, indeed, the best course to follow, he or she will explain to you the two options available. An individual could file either a Chapter 7 or a Chapter 13 (a third option, Chapter 11, is used primarily by businesses).

We will go into each option in more detail in later chapters, but briefly, Chapter 7 is your right under the Federal Bankruptcy Act to clear yourself of debt and began all over again, while Chapter 13 is a legal procedure under the same act to help those people in unmanageable debt to pay all or part of their debts under the protection of the U.S. Bankruptcy Courts. The difference between the two is that under Chapter 7, you can be released from debts by paying only a fraction of what you owe, or even nothing, while Chapter 13 was enacted to enable debtors to meet their financial obligations, albeit over a prolonged period of time.

Bankruptcy Information Forms

After explaining the alternatives, the attorney should then advise you as to which option is best for you. When the choice is made, the attorney will provide you with the proper bankruptcy information form (either for Chapter 7 or Chapter 13—there is a sample of each in the appendixes). You must take this form home, fill it out completely, and then return it to the attorney. The attorney will then review it to make sure you have filled it out properly and completely. For instance, failure to list certain creditors might result in fraud, whereby nullifying the bankruptcy proceeding.

This information sheet serves several functions. Among other things, it allows the attorney to:

1. Check all your creditors for possible conflicts with office clients, either past or present.
2. Check to see what assets are nonexempt.
3. Check for problems with dischargeability of debt, objections to discharge, preferences, and fraudulent and other avoidable transfers.
4. Check income and budget statements to see the extent to which you may require counsel on a Chapter 13 bankruptcy proceeding.
5. Verify to the court that all subjects have been covered.

After reviewing the form, the attorney will then prepare a petition in which each creditor is named. When the petition is submitted to the court, you should stop paying all unsecured creditors (secured loans, such as car or house payments, should still be paid, otherwise you will lose that property) except for the necessities—rent, telephone, electricity, and the like.

Appearing in Court

A court date will then be set for approximately forty days later (depending on the backlog, it could take up to four to six months). The court will notify all your creditors, giving them the opportunity to face you and raise any questions regarding your debts. Rarely, however, do they actually appear.

In court, you will appear in front of a trustee in bankruptcy. Usually this is an attorney. He or she will review your bankruptcy petition and usually ask a number of questions, such as: Do you have any assets? Are you owed any money? Are you expecting a tax refund? He or she will usually ask to see your last two tax returns (bring these with you).

Once you have answered all questions to the satisfaction of the judge, the meeting is closed.

If you continue to be harassed by bill collectors, or there is an income garnishment on your salary, either you should notify these creditors that you have filed bankruptcy (you can do this by writing a letter in which you should include your court docket number, saying that all your debts have been discharged by the court); or you may ask your attorney to contact your creditor.

The Discharge Hearing

Two or three months later (again, this time period may vary, even taking as much as up to a year), you will be notified of what's known as your discharge hearing. If you have filed under Chapter 7, in most cases you will not have to appear in court, unless any of your creditors have objected to the discharge of your debts due to fraud. Rather, the hearing is simply a formality to reaffirm the judgment of the court. If you have filed under Chapter 13, however, you must appear.

Once this hearing has taken place and the court has affirmed the discharge of your debts, you may begin over with a clean financial slate.

Six Most Commonly Asked Questions

1. *What is the difference between filing for bankruptcy under Chapter 7 and Chapter 13?*

Chapter 7 is available to those who wish to discharge all their debts and start over again, while Chapter 13 is a reorganization procedure in which creditors are paid all or a portion of what the debtor owes over an extended period of time and receive a discharge from the balance due.

2. *I have decided to file for bankruptcy, but there are some debts I would like to repay and would therefore like to list on the bankruptcy form. Can I do this?*

If you fail to list all your creditors, you may be guilty of fraud. If your bankruptcy petition is challenged by one creditor on this basis, it is possible that you will be denied the opportunity to obtain a discharge.

3. *I have filed for bankruptcy but I continue to get dunning letters from creditors. Is there anything I can do?*

Either you can write a letter informing your creditors of the bankruptcy proceeding (include the docket number of your case), or you can have your attorney write a letter.

4. *How long does the entire bankruptcy procedure take?*

From the time you visit your attorney and make the decision to file until the time your case is discharged should take somewhere between four to six months.

5. *If I file for bankruptcy, how many times will I have to appear in court?*

Once for sure, at the first court date set, at which time all your creditors will have the opportunity to appear. However, few if any of your creditors will actually appear. You may have to appear a second time (in some states your appearance is mandatory) at your discharge hearing, but unless any of your creditors files an objection, this is rather unlikely.

Following is a brief chronological outline of how we at Jacoby & Meyers handle the average bankruptcy case:

1. The client is given a bankruptcy information form (either a Chapter 7 or a Chapter 13), which he or she will be asked to take home and fill out.

2. The client returns with the completed bankruptcy information form. It is reviewed to see that it has been filled out properly.

3. The attorney fills out and mails the appropriate form to the Bankruptcy Unit of the court. The Bankruptcy Unit responds, usually within a day, by sending a petition to the attorney.

4. The client returns to the office and signs the petition. The petition is then returned to the Bankruptcy Unit.

5. The court usually files the petition within several weeks of its return. The court schedules the first meeting of creditors approximately forty days after filing. The court notifies the debtor, the creditors, and the attorney of the date.

6. The first meeting usually takes five or ten minutes. Questions the trustee asks are similar to those on the bankruptcy information form. Usually, though not always, this will be your only appearance in court.

7. Approximately four months after the first meeting is held, a discharge notice is sent out, and the proceeding is completed.

6. *If I file for bankruptcy and the day after my case is closed I win $1 million in the lottery, do I have to repay my previous debts?*

You might feel a moral obligation to repay your debts, but you have absolutely no legal obligation, because your debts were discharged by the bankruptcy proceeding.

4

FILING UNDER CHAPTER 7

Once you've reached the conclusion that you are insolvent (which means that your debts are greater than your assets and that you have no realistic hope of paying them off) and decide to file bankruptcy, you should take several steps.

First, you must stop making any purchases on credit. You must pay back any purchases over $500 that you make during the twenty days prior to filing. If you continue to run up bills on your credit card while you are in the process of filing bankruptcy, you may be charged with fraud.

If you have a loan with the same bank where you have a checking account (which would mean that the bank is also a creditor), you should also stop using your checking account. Once checks already issued have cleared, you should close the account.

As part of your bankruptcy plan, your attorney may also advise you to take steps to convert nonexempt assets into exempt assets. For instance, if you have a few hundred dollars in cash, it might be a good idea to purchase something for your home that would fall under one of the appropriate exemptions.

Although these conversions may later be challenged during the bankruptcy proceeding, many legal experts maintain this action is allowable. However, as a general rule, any assets that are converted within ninety days of filing the bankruptcy petition are subject to being challenged. For this reason, it's especially crucial that you consult an attorney before making any conversions.

How It Works

Traditional bankruptcy, also known as "Liquidation Bankruptcy," is your right under Chapter 7 of the Federal Bankruptcy Act to clear yourself of all debt and start over again. Chapter 7 was designed for individuals and businesses that want to make a fresh start but are unable to pay their debts from their current income.

When filing under Chapter 7, you are allowed to exempt, or keep, certain property. Whatever property remains is turned over to a court-appointed trustee to be liquidated (sold). After the assets have been converted into cash, the trustee deducts the administrative fees and then distributes the remainder to your creditors in payment of your debts. If you have either no or few nonexempt assets, it is possible that your debts can be discharged without your having to pay anything.

Although you may file for Chapter 7 without the help of an attorney, we strongly advise against doing so. A good attorney knows when and how to file the proper papers and can also help you formulate a workable exemption plan that can go a long way in helping you keep as many of your assets as possible, while at the same time avoiding any possible charges of fraud.

Chapter 7 begins with the filing of a petition, schedules of assets and liabilities, and a statement of financial affairs with the bankruptcy court that serves the area where the individual debtor lives or where the business debtor has its main office.

A husband and wife may file one joint petition. A filing fee to cover court costs, currently ranging from $120 and up, is to be paid upon filing. However, with the court's permission, individuals may pay this fee in up to four installments. Failure to pay the fee may result in either dismissal of the case or a delay in receiving discharge. If a joint petition is filed, only one $120 fee is charged.

Once the petition is filed and the fee is paid, an impartial trustee is appointed by the court or the United States Trustee to administer the case and liquidate your nonexempt assets.

Who May File?

Most individuals have the right to file a Chapter 7 bankruptcy. It was designed for those with little or no income beyond that which is necessary to pay for food, shelter, and other necessities.

However, an individual may not file if, during the preceding 180 days, a prior bankruptcy petition was dismissed as a result of the debtor's failure to appear or comply with the orders of the court; or if a petition was dismissed after creditors sought permission from the bankruptcy court to recover property upon which they hold liens.

The court has the right to dismiss a Chapter 7 case filed by an individual whose debts are primarily the result of consumer purchases rather than business debts, if the court finds that the debtor is substantially abusing the provisions of the act.

The court may also deny a discharge of debts if the debtor has received a discharge in a previous Chapter 7 case within the past six years.

Even if you obtain a discharge, there are some debts that are not dischargeable under the law. These debts include certain taxes, student loans, alimony and support payments, debts fraudulently incurred, debts for willful and malicious injury to persons or property, and debts arising from a drunken driving judgment.

The Bankruptcy Information Form

Before the Chapter 7 bankruptcy petition can be filed, your attorney may give you a bankruptcy information form. You should take this form home and fill it out completely and accurately. If it is not filled out properly, your bankruptcy petition could be dismissed.

This form includes a list of all creditors; a list of all your property; and a detailed list of your monthly income and living expenses, which would include food, clothing, shelter, utilities, taxes, transportation, medicine, insurance, and so on. An example of a typical Chapter 7 bankruptcy form appears in appendix A.

After you complete the form, return it to your attorney, who will review it with you. At the same time, you should bring the following items with you:

1. Deeds, mortgages, contracts on your home, and mortgage statements.
2. Any papers relating to past bankruptcies and wage earners' plans to repay debts (Chapter 13).
3. Copies of all tax returns for the past two years.
4. All legal papers, which would include summonses, complaints, notices of attachments and executions, and so on, pertaining to your credit problems.
5. Statement and passbooks for savings or checking accounts for the past twelve months.

Exemptions

The purpose of the bankruptcy law is not to strip you of all assets and leave you destitute with little else but the shirt on your back, but rather to allow you to rid yourself of burdensome debt and start over.

Consequently, under the Federal Bankruptcy Act certain kinds of property are exempt from liquidation. Approximately thirty-five states, however, have adopted their own exemption law to be used in place of the federal exemptions. In many cases the state laws are less liberal than the federal law, while Texas, Florida, and California are far more lenient in what property they permit to be exempt. Consequently, the nature and value of property—such as a house, car, clothes, jewelry—that is exempt is dependent on the law of the individual state in which you reside. For this reason, it's best to consult a local attorney to find out just what exemptions your state allows.

Federal Exemptions

Following is a list of the major exemptions under the Federal Bankruptcy Act.

- Your home (as residence, otherwise the exemption is only $3,750) or your personal property—up to a value of $7,500. You may distribute this exemption in any way between your home and your personal property, which might include a burial plot, land, trailer, motor vehicle, or business inventory. If you do not own a home, you can apply the full exemption to your personal property. (For comparison's sake, the State of California offers a couple an exemption of up to $75,000 on a homestead, while the federal exemption for a couple would only be $15,000.)
- One motor vehicle, up to the value of $1,200.
- Household or personal property, which includes books, appliances, musical instruments, and animals, up to a value of $4,000 per household.
- Jewelry, up to a value of $500.
- Professional books or tools of the trade, up to a value of $750.
- The cash value of insurance policies, up to a value of $4,000.
- Additional property, such as bank accounts, tax refunds, and anticipated tax refunds, up to a value of $400.
- Compensation for injury or losses, such as a settlement received for bodily injury.
- The following forms of income: the most common kinds of Social Security benefits, disability benefits, local public assistance benefits, unemployment compensation, pension fund payments, profit-

sharing plan payments, life insurance benefits, income from annuities, alimony, support or separate maintenance, veterans' benefits, and any anticipated future income.

In some states, both spouses need not choose the same system of exemptions. For instance, a husband can choose the federal exemption rules, while his wife may choose the state's rules. However, once you've chosen the particular system, you must follow it throughout. In other words, you can't choose the federal exemption for housing and then the state for jewelry.

State Exemptions

Following are examples of some of the state exemptions you may be allowed.

MASSACHUSETTS

- Cemeteries and burial property—rights of burial and tombs are exempt.
- Homestead or residential property—in most cases, $100,000 in principal family residence is exempt.
- Public assistance—you may exempt any money received by or owed as public assistance; aid to dependent children is specifically exempt.
- Motor vehicles—you may exempt an automobile worth up to $750 and necessary for personal transportation or to maintain employment.

INDIANA

- Crime victim's compensation—exempt, unless a creditor's claim is included in the award.
- Pension and retirement benefits—various pension benefits for public employees are exempt.

CALIFORNIA

- Building materials—you may exempt $1,000 in materials for improvement of your principal place of residence.

NEW YORK

- Library materials—school books and other books not exceeding $50 in value are exempt.

Notification

Once your petition has been filed, the court will notify your creditors. At this time, most actions taken by creditors to collect money owed them must stop. By law, creditors cannot initiate or continue any lawsuits, wage garnishments, or even telephone calls demanding payment after they receive notice that you have filed for bankruptcy.

The Meeting of Creditors

After the petition is filed, a date will be assigned for a "meeting of creditors" to be held. As the debtor, you must attend this meeting, along with any creditors who want to ask questions regarding your financial affairs and property. (In most cases, the creditors do not attend. If a husband and wife have filed jointly, they must both attend this meeting.) The trustee assigned to the case, who is usually an attorney, will also attend and will question you on your financial affairs.

It is essential that you cooperate with the trustee and provide any financial records or documents that he or she requests.

In order to preserve their independent judgment, bankruptcy judges are prohibited from attending the creditors' meeting.

Discharge

Approximately three to four months after the creditors' meeting, you will receive a discharge, which absolves you of the obligation to pay any debts that cannot be paid by the trustee after your nonexempt assets have been liquidated.

Generally speaking, unsecured debts are obligations that are based solely on the future ability to pay, as opposed to secured debts, which are based not only on the ability to pay but also the creditor's right to seize pledged property upon default. (The mortgage on a house and a car loan are examples of secured loans.)

Those creditors whose unsecured debts are discharged may no longer initiate or continue any legal or other action against you to collect on obligations. However, secured creditors retain some rights that may permit them to seize pledged property, even after a discharge is granted.

For this reason, it is often advantageous for you to "reaffirm" a debt when property, such as a car, has been pledged to the creditor. A reaffirmation is an agreement between the debtor and the creditor that the debtor will pay the money owed, even though he or she filed for bankruptcy. In return for this agreement, the creditor promises that as long as payments are made, the car or other property will not be repossessed.

You must file this written reaffirmation agreement with the court. If you are not represented by an attorney, the agreement must be approved by the judge before you are discharged. We strongly advise that, if you are considering a reaffirmation agreement, you consult an attorney. He or she will not only advise you as to whether such an agreement is in your best interests but will see to it that your rights are fully protected.

Even though your debts are discharged under Chapter 7, any cosigners or codebtors you may have are not relieved of their responsibility. Consequently creditors can still collect from them.

Once again, there are certain nondischargeable debts, which include the following:

- Alimony, maintenance, and child support obligations.
- Most taxes due within the past three years, unless you filed no return. Some taxes are dischargeable after a period of time. To find out which ones, consult your attorney.
- Debts arising from credit obtained by providing false information concerning your financial situation.
- Fines or penalties payable to the government, including tax penalties and fines for traffic violations.
- Payments on student loans unless they have been due and unpaid for five years, or unless repayment would cause substantial hardship. However, in some federal court districts these unpaid student loans are dischargeable by paying a percentage of the debt. Some student loans are never dischargeable.
- Other debts that the court might designate as nondischargeable as the result of legal proceedings brought by the creditors.

Denial or Revocation

The bankruptcy procedure is based on truth. Should any kind of fraud be discovered, such as the debtor hiding assets or failing to obey a lawful order of the court, the discharge can be denied or revoked.

Bankruptcy fraud is a felony under federal criminal law and may result in arrest, fine, or imprisonment.

Effects on Your Future Credit

Once your bankruptcy petition has been registered by the court, the major consumer credit reporting agencies will automatically record it in their files. This information will remain on file for ten years.

Practically speaking, this means that every time you want to make a purchase on credit, the creditor will check your file and be informed of your bankruptcy petition. As you can imagine, this is not the kind of thing creditors like to see, and it often leads to denying credit.

Nevertheless, you may be able to talk to the individual creditor and explain the reasons that caused you to file— perhaps a serious illness or the loss of a job. If you have a reasonably good, steady income at the time and you've been able to put some money in the bank, you may be able to persuade the lender to extend you some credit.

One thing you might try in the case of a bank is to offer to deposit $1,000 in a savings account, promising to leave it there indefinitely. In return, you could ask for a credit card with a limit of $1,000, which would be backed by that savings account.

Obtaining credit after filing bankruptcy might also depend on the plan you choose. For instance, because you may not file for Chapter 7 more than once every six years, you may actually be a good credit risk, as by law you cannot go into bankruptcy again for six years.

But the best way to obtain credit again is to pay all your bills on time. With this sort of recent performance, some places might issue you credit. This way, slowly but surely, you can build up an acceptable credit rating.

Five Most Commonly Asked Questions

1. *I have filed for Chapter 7 bankruptcy, but I still have a charge card on which I haven't reached my credit limit. May I still use it?*

   No. Once you've filed bankruptcy you should stop making purchases on credit. And any purchases made for over $500 during the twenty days prior to filing must be repaid.

2. *I would like to file bankruptcy, but I'm afraid that all my assets will be taken and I'll be left destitute. Is this the case?*

   No. The purpose of the bankruptcy law is to allow debtors to discharge most debts and start over again, not to punish them and leave them penniless. Consequently, the law provides for various exemptions from liquidation.

3. *I cosigned a loan for my brother-in-law and he has filed bankruptcy. Am I off the hook?*

   No. As a cosigner, you are still responsible and the creditor may come after you.

4. *I have filed bankruptcy. One of my debts is $3,000 worth of maintenance and child support money due my ex-wife. Will I have to pay that?*

   Certain debts are nondischargeable. Child support and maintenance fall under that category.

5. *After I've filed bankruptcy is there anyway I can obtain credit before the ten years that it will appear on my credit rating have passed?*

   Certainly potential creditors will be wary of you, but if you have shown you are a good risk by paying your bills on time for a year or so, you may be able to obtain credit once again.

5

FILING UNDER CHAPTER 13

Filing under Chapter 7 allows debtors to be released from their debts by paying only a fraction of what they owe, or even nothing at all. On the other hand, Chapter 13 of the Federal Bankruptcy Act allows the debtor who wants to meet his or her financial obligations to do so in a manageable way.

In short, Chapter 13 was designed for those debtors who have a regular income and who wish to pay their debts but are currently unable to make full payment. The primary benefit of Chapter 13 relief is the ability to repay creditors, either in full or in part, in installments spread out over a three- to five-year period. During this time creditors are barred from starting or continuing collecting efforts, or foreclosing on property.

How It Works

As soon as you file under Chapter 13, all legal action brought against you as a result of your debts must stop, and any future action of this type is prohibited.

Your creditors are forbidden to telephone you, write you, appear personally, dun you, or make any kind of attempt to collect money from you.

Garnishments cannot be made against you, and any that have already been made must be terminated. You are entitled to receive your full wages, without any deductions from your creditors.

Your creditors are barred from contacting your employer in any way.

Any late charges, service charges, and in some cases interest charges must be discontinued.

In some cases where you have any cosigners or codebtors, all collection attempts and garnishments against them are stopped. This action prevents losses from damaging your relations with friends and relatives who underwrote some of your obligations. However, if your creditors apply to the court to lift this barring of action against cosigners, the cosigners remain liable for the debt even though you may eventually be released from it.

Creditors are barred from repossessing property or seizing property put up as collateral.

A Chapter 13 case begins with the filing of a petition, schedules of assets and liabilities, and a statement of financial affairs with the bankruptcy court serving the area where you reside.

You will need to provide the following information:

- A list of all creditors
- The source, amount, frequency, and reliability of your income
- A list of all your property
- A detailed list of your monthly living expenses, including food, clothing, shelter, utilities, taxes, transportation, and medicine.

Who May File?

You are eligible to file under Chapter 13 (originally called "wage earner bankruptcy") if you are an individual wage earner, small business owner (corporations cannot qualify as Chapter 13 debtors), or a professional (except for stockbrokers and commodities dealers), with a regular income and unsecured debts under $100,000 and secured debts under $350,000.

A husband and wife may file one joint petition.

If, during the preceding 180 days, a bankruptcy petition has been dismissed due to your failure to appear or comply with orders of the court, you may not file under Chapter 13.

The Bankruptcy Information Form

You must fill out the bankruptcy information form provided by your attorney, with all the pertinent information. It is important that you fill it out completely and accurately. If you do not do so, your petition may be denied on the grounds of fraud. An example of a typical Chapter 13 bankruptcy form appears in appendix B.

If a husband and wife file a single, joint petition, they should be prepared to provide this detailed information for both spouses. However, even when only one spouse files, the income and expenses of the nonfiling spouse should be included.

The filing fee to cover court costs is currently $90. You may pay this fee in full upon filing or, with the court's permission, you may pay it in up to four installments. If a joint petition is filed, only one $90 fee is charged.

After You File

Once you file your petition, a trustee is appointed by a federal court. Within fifteen days after filing you must submit a plan of repayment that has been devised by you and your attorney. The trustee will review this plan. If it is approved, it will be submitted to the court as a way of paying all your creditors over a period of three to five years. The plan should provide for payments of fixed amounts to the trustee on a regular basis, either biweekly or monthly.

A judge of the bankruptcy court will then approve the plan. Once approval is obtained, the trustee will then distribute the funds to creditors according to the terms of the plan. As the payments are stretched out over a longer period of time, your monthly payments may decrease, thus making it easier for you to pay off your debts.

If it is determined that you do not have enough disposable income (income not reasonably necessary for the maintenance or support of you and your dependents) to pay off your creditors in full, you will then be obligated to commit to the proposed plan all projected disposable income over the next three to five years that the plan is in effect. In this case, the trustee may arrange for you to pay only a portion of the debt, which may amount to only a small percentage of what you actually owe. When that portion is paid, your debts are considered completely cleared.

You may request a five-year plan rather than a three-year plan, but unless you can show "good cause" for extending the time of your payments, the trustee will recommend, and the judge will most likely approve, the shorter plan.

Within thirty days after you file your plan with the court, even though it has not yet been officially approved, you must begin making payments to the trustee.

Approximately twenty to forty days after your petition is filed, a meeting of creditors is held. You must attend this meeting, at which creditors may appear and ask questions regarding your financial affairs and the proposed terms of the plan. If you have filed with your spouse, both of you must attend. Your trustee will be there and will also question you on your financial affairs. However, the bankruptcy judge will not attend, in order that he or she can maintain impartiality.

If there are any problems with your repayment plan, they are usually resolved during or shortly after the creditors' meetings.

The kinds of objections that might be raised include the complaint that payments offered under the plan are less than the creditors would receive if your assets were liquidated and that your plan fails to commit all extra income for the three to five years that the plan is in effect.

If your debts are unsecured, meaning there is no property held as collateral, your creditors must accept the payments decreed by the court, provided that under Chapter 13 they would receive more than if you filed under Chapter 7.

Approval of Your Plan

If your plan is approved by the bankruptcy judge, the trustee begins to distribute the funds that you have been paying. If the plan is not approved the funds that you have paid to the trustee are returned to you after deducting the trustee's costs, which are authorized by the court. At this time you must come up with another plan.

If your ability to pay has been altered or if you've inadvertently left certain creditors out of your plan, it is possible to modify the plan either before or after it's been approved.

Making It Work

Once your plan has been approved by the court, you must follow it. You are required to make regular payments to the trustee. This means that you will have to live on a fixed budget for the duration of the plan. You should also be very careful not to incur any significant credit obligations without first consulting the trustee, as these obligations may affect the execution of your plan.

One thing you can do to make sure that you follow your plan is to have the plan payments deducted from your paycheck. This may increase the likelihood that the payments will be made on time.

If you do fail to make the proper payments, your case may be dismissed. It will be converted to a liquidation proceeding under Chapter 7 of the Bankruptcy Code.

Discharge

When your plan is finally completed—that is, when you have honored all your obligations—you will receive a discharge that exonerates you from your obligations to pay any unsecured debts that were included in the plan but were not paid in full through it. Generally speaking, unsecured debts are those that are based solely on your future ability to pay. Secured debts are based upon a creditor's right to seize on default any property that you've pledged as collateral.

As a rule, all debts are discharged under Chapter 13 except:

- Alimony and support obligations
- Certain taxes
- Certain secured obligations.

These debts must be paid for in full under a plan.

In return for your willingness to undergo the discipline of a three- to five-year repayment plan, a broader discharge encompassing a greater range of debts is provided than is available if you'd filed a Chapter 7 Bankruptcy.

Hardship Discharges

After the court approves your bankruptcy plan, you may request the court to grant you a "hardship discharge" in certain circumstances. As a rule, these discharges are available to you only if your failure to complete your plan payments is due to circumstances beyond your control and if your creditors have already received at least as much as they would have received under a Chapter 7 liquidation proceeding. Injury or illness that affects your employment may constitute one reason for such a hardship discharge. Such a discharge is only a viable alternative when a modification plan is impossible.

Five Most Commonly Asked Questions

1. *Can Chapter 13 help me from defaulting on my mortgage?*

   Yes. While you continue to make regular monthly payments, you can spread out payments of arrears, which would include late charges and interest, over eighteen months to five years, according to your court-approved plan. It is rare to obtain permission to spread out arrears for more than three years, but it is possible. As long as you comply with the terms of your mortgage, there can be no foreclosure.

2. *I owe some tax money. Is there any way I can obtain relief under a Chapter 13 Bankruptcy?*

   Both back and current taxes may be paid off during the life of your plan, provided they're paid in full with interest.

3. *How do my attorney and I determine how much I can afford to pay each month under my Chapter 13 plan?*

   You must figure out how much money you have available each month after you've paid for your necessities, which include food, shelter, clothing, and so on. This sum is then split among your creditors.

4. *Can my creditors refuse to accept partial payment of my debts?*

   If your debts are unsecured, then your creditors must accept the payments decreed by the court, provided that under Chapter 13 they would receive more than under Chapter 7.

5. *When I first filed Bankruptcy under Chapter 13, I was able to make my monthly payments. But now, due to a prolonged illness, I am unemployed. Is there anything I can do?*

   Yes. You may file for a hardship discharge, which might be granted, but only if the creditors have already received at least as much as they would have received if you'd filed under Chapter 7.

APPENDIX A

Chapter 7 Bankruptcy
Information Form

The Bankruptcy Court requires the information requested by the questions contained in this form. *Complete answers are necessary before we can file your bankruptcy papers with the Court.*
YOU MUST INCLUDE ACCOUNT NUMBERS FOR EVERY CREDITOR.

Instructions

1. Answer completely EACH question on EVERY page. When you are given a choice of YES or NO, circle the correct answer. If your answer is YES, give the information which is requested.

2. PRINT CLEARLY or TYPEWRITE your answers. We MUST be able to read your answers.

3. Where the name and address of a person or company is asked for, give the full name and complete address *INCLUDING THE ZIP CODE.* Be sure the address and zip code are correct. For zip code information, phone 212/971–7411. For an address outside of the New York area, dial the area code of the city you want + 555–1212 (the operator can provide you with an area code). The long distance information (Area Code + 555–1212) can provide you with the phone number of the person or company you are seeking, and possibly an address. If long distance information cannot provide you with an address, you can call the number given and ask the person or company their exact address, including zip code.

NOTE: An incorrect or incomplete address may prevent discharge (cancellation) of your debt.

4. If you do not know the exact amount you owe a creditor, fill in an estimate.

5. If you do not understand a question, put a question mark by it, and discuss it with the attorney when you bring back this form.

6. If you need more space to answer a question, write "SEE ATTACHED" when you run out of space on the form, and continue your answer on a separate piece of paper. Write the number of the question on the paper and attach it to this form.

FULL NAME—NO INITIALS

First	Middle	Last	

Present Address	City	State	Zip Code

Home Number	Work Number	Social Security Number

SCHEDULE A-1
Debts Having Priority

a. & b. If you employed anyone (such as regular employees, cleaning women, gardeners, babysitters) during the last three (3) months, do you still owe him or her wages?
[ ] YES [ ] NO

If YES, give the name and address of employee, amount owed, the date worked for which you owe, the employee wages and type of work done. Also, give amounts owed for contributions to employment benefit plan during last six months.

SCHEDULE A-2
SECURED DEBTS

Do you owe money to a creditor who has an interest in some item of your property, which they can take if you do not pay them (such as car loans, home mortgages, etc.)? The complete address of the creditor must be given. If you have refinanced the loan, give the last date you refinanced it.

BE CERTAIN TO LIST ANY AGENCIES THAT MAY GUARANTEE YOUR LOAN (F.H.A., VA, ETC.)

NAME, ADDRESS OF CREDITORS AND ACCOUNT NUMBERS	WHAT DEBT IS FOR	WHAT PROPERTY CAN BE TAKEN IF YOU FAIL TO PAY DEBT	MONTH AND YEAR MONEY FIRST OWED	VALUE OF PROPERTY	LOCATION OF PROPERTY	HOW MUCH DO YOU OWE	CIRCLE ONE
							SURRENDER/ REDEEM/ REAFFIRM
							SURRENDER/ REDEEM/ REAFFIRM

DEFINITIONS: Surrender—I desire to turn secured asset over to creditor.
    Redeem —I desire to make a lump sum payment to creditor equal to value of asset.
    Reaffirm —I desire to continue my current monthly payments and retain asset and to continue to be obligated to creditor after I am discharged.

SCHEDULE A-3
UNSECURED DEBTS

List by name of original creditor ALL debts where no goods can be taken by the creditor (such as doctor bills, credit cards). Also include here any debts for which you have cosigned that are not paid in full. Also list names and addresses of who cosigned for you.

NAME OF ORIGINAL CREDITOR	BILLING ADDRESS OF ORIGINAL CREDITOR (NOT COLLECTION AGENCY ACCOUNT NUMBERS)	WHAT DEBT IS FOR	MONTH AND YEAR OF DEBT. IF CHARGE ACCOUNT, DATE OF FIRST PURCHASE AND DATE OF LAST PURCHASE	AMOUNT OWING

c. Have you given any money as deposit toward purchase or rental of property or services for personal, family, or household use that were not provided or delivered?
[ ] YES [ ] NO
If YES, give name and address of person or business to whom deposit was given, amount of deposit, and property or services for which deposit was made.

1. Do you owe any taxes to the U.S. Government?
   [ ] YES [ ] NO
   If YES, give the name and address of the department or agency to which the tax is owing, the amount and kind of tax that is owing and the years for which tax is owing.

   _____

2. Do you owe any taxes to any state?
   [ ] YES [ ] NO
   If YES, give the name and address of the department or agency to which the tax is owing, the amount and kind of tax that is owing and the years for which tax is owing.

   _____

3. Do you owe any taxes to a county, special district or city?
   [ ] YES [ ] NO
   If YES, give the name and address of the department or agency to which the tax is owing, the amount and kind of tax that is owing and the years for which tax is owing.

   _____

SCHEDULE B-1

Do you own your own home, any land, co-op, condominium? [ ] YES [ ] NO
If YES, give address and bring in any papers related to your

interest (for example, mortgages, deeds, title insurance, contracts, mortgage statement).

If you own your home, please give:
Date of Purchase ——————— Purchase Price —————
Amount of Down Payment —————————————
Amount now owed on first mortgage —————————
Amount now owed on second mortgage ————————
Estimate of present fair market value ————————

Is your mortgage guaranteed by any federal or state agency?
[ ] YES   [ ] NO

Name and relationship to you of anyone whose name is on the deed.

SCHEDULE B-2

a. How much cash do you have on hand (not in banks)?
    —————

b. How much of a rent security does your landlord hold?——

c. Do you now have money deposited anywhere (bank checking or savings, savings and loan association, credit union)?
    [ ] YES   [ ] NO
    If YES, give the following:

NAME OF BANK OR INSTITUTION	CHECKING OR SAVINGS	AMOUNT NOW ON DEPOSIT

d. Estimate the value (what you could get if you had to sell quickly) of all your furniture and all your appliances

$_____. Describe any SINGLE item of your furniture or appliances worth more than $200.00.

e. Have you any rare books, prints, paintings or pictures of value?
[ ] YES [ ] NO
If YES, give the value of all your books $_____
and the value of all your prints, paintings and pictures
$_____.

f. Estimate the value (what you could get if you had to sell quickly) for all of your clothing $_____, all your jewelry $_____, all your firearms and sports equipment $_____.

g. Do you have any vehicles (autos, trucks, tractors, motor bikes, trailers, etc.)? [ ] YES [ ] NO If YES give:

YEAR	MAKE	MODEL	MARKET VALUE	AMOUNT OWING

h. Do you have any boats, motors or their accessories?
[ ] YES [ ] NO
If YES, indicate value $_____, and describe: _____

i. Do you have any horses, cows, sheep, or other animals? (Do not include pets unless valuable.)
[ ] YES [ ] NO
If YES, indicate value $_____, and describe: _____

j. Do you have any crops or farming equipment?
[ ] YES [ ] NO
If YES, indicate value $_____, and describe: _____

k. Do you have any office equipment, furnishings or supplies?
[ ] YES [ ] NO
If YES, indicate value $_____, and describe: _____

l. Do you have any machinery, fixtures, or tools used in your business or occupation (other than those listed in items k and m)?
[ ] YES [ ] NO
If YES, indicate value $_____, and describe: _____

_____

m. Do you have any stock in trade (inventory) from any business?
[ ] YES [ ] NO
If YES, indicate the value $_____, and describe:

_____

n. Do you have anything of value not listed above that could be considered a piece of property, real or personal?
[ ] YES [ ] NO
If YES, indicate value $_____, and describe:

_____

o. Do you have any patents, copyrights, trademarks, or franchises?
[ ] YES [ ] NO
If YES, indicate value $_____, and describe:

_____

p. Do you have any government or other type of bonds?
[ ] YES [ ] NO
If YES, indicate value $_____, and describe: _____

_____

q. Does anyone owe you money?   [ ] YES [ ] NO
   If YES, indicate their name, address, and amount they
   owe you:

   _____

r. Are you owed, or do you intend to sue anyone, for
   personal injury, or money owed to you or other members
   of your family?
   [ ] YES [ ] NO
   If YES, describe and give amounts you are suing or will
   sue for:

   _____

   _____

s. Do you have any life insurance policies?
   [ ] YES [ ] NO
   If YES, list the following (if you have a small life and health
   policy through job or union, simply state "Life and Health
   through employer"):

NAME OF INSURANCE COMPANY	TYPE OF POLICY	ANNUAL PREMIUM	CANCELLATION OR SURRENDER VALUE

t. Do you have any interest in an annuity?
   [ ] YES [ ] NO
   If YES, indicate value $_____, and describe: _____

u. Do you have any stocks or bonds? [ ] YES [ ] NO
   If YES, indicate value $_____, and describe: _____

v. Do you have any interest in a partnership?
   [ ] YES [ ] NO
   If YES, indicate value $_____, and describe: _____

w.   Are you a holder of any future power of interest in real property or is any real property being held for you by someone else?
[ ] YES   [ ] NO
If YES, indicate value $_____, and describe: _____

SCHEDULE B-3

a.   Have you transferred any property for the benefit of all your creditors?   [ ] YES   [ ] NO
IF YES, give a description of the property, its value and date of transfer: _____

b.   Do you have any other property, land or personal property not already listed?   [ ] YES   [ ] NO
If YES, indicate value $_____, and describe: _____

c.   Does your spouse or do your children have anything of value not listed above?   [ ] YES   [ ] NO
If YES, indicate value $_____, and describe: _____

STATEMENT OF AFFAIRS

What county do you live in? _____

How long have you lived there? ____ years ____ months.

1.   a.   Full name (no initials) _____
                                  FIRST   MIDDLE   LAST

_____
SOCIAL SECURITY NUMBER

b.   PRINT other names you have been known by during the last SIX YEARS. _____

c & d.   List all the addresses where you have lived during the last six years, 72 months, along with the dates you lived at each location. _____

2. a. What is your occupation? _____

    b. Are you employed? _____. Give the name
        and address of your employer and the date you began
        work:

        _____

        _____

    c. Have you been in business during the last six years?
        [ ] YES   [ ] NO

        If YES, attach a separate sheet of paper and give the
        name and address of each business, the dates of
        operation, and the names and addresses of the other
        partners, if any, for EACH business you were in. List
        all assets of each business and indicate whether they
        are still operating.

d & e. List income received during the last TWO years by
        you and your spouse from any source. (List your
        spouse's income only if you were living together dur-
        ing the period of time required by the questions.)

SOURCE OF INCOME	19___		19___	
	YOU	SPOUSE	YOU	SPOUSE
WAGES-SALARY (NOT TAKE HOME)				
WELFARE BENEFITS				
SOCIAL SECURITY BENEFITS				
UNEMPLOYMENT BENEFITS				

RETIREMENT OR PENSION   _____

   Describe: _____

VETERANS BENEFITS   _____

CHILD SUPPORT YOU RECEIVED   _____

YOUR INHERITANCE   _____

   Describe: _____

WORKMAN'S COMPENSATION OR OTHER   _____
MONEY YOU RECOVERED FOR
DISABILITY OR INJURY   _____

   Describe: _____

OTHER INCOME: _____

   Describe: _____

---

3. a. To what city and state did you SEND your TWO last FEDERAL and STATE Income Tax Returns, and for what years were they filed? Give the city and state to which each form was mailed.

	CITY	STATE	YEAR TAX RETURN MAILED	YEAR FOR WHICH RETURN FILED
FEDERAL:				
STATE:				

LAST RETURN FILED

NEXT TO LAST   FEDERAL: _____
RETURN FILED

STATE: _____

   b. Give the amount of tax refunds you received last year:

      FEDERAL: $_____ STATE: $_____

   c. To what tax refunds are you entitled? _____
If you have already prepared your return, amount claimed:

      FEDERAL: $_____ STATE: $_____

4. a. Have you had a bank account (savings or checking, Credit Union, Christmas Club, Savings and Loan Account) or any other type of deposit of money by yourself or with another person during the last 24 months? [ ] YES [ ] NO

NAME OF BANK	COMPLETE ADDRESS	TYPE: CHECKING OR SAVINGS	AMOUNT: OPEN OR CLOSED	NAME OF OTHER PERSON WHO COULD MAKE WITHDRAWALS ON ACCOUNT

   b. Have you had a safe deposit box during the last 24 months?
[ ] YES [ ] NO If YES, state:

NAME OF BANK OR INSTITUTION	BRANCH	BRIEF DESCRIPTION OF CONTENTS	DATE BOX CLOSED, IF CLOSED	NAME OF PERSONS WHO COULD ENTER

5. a. Have you kept records or books relating to your affairs during the last TWO years? [ ] YES [ ] NO

    b. If YES, who has these records or books? _____

c & d. Describe any records or books that have been lost or thrown away and give dates on which they were lost or thrown away:

_____

6. Do you have any property that is not yours, that you are holding for someone else? [ ] YES [ ] NO

7. Have you or your spouse ever filed a bankruptcy or Chapter 13 wage earner's plan? [ ] YES [ ] NO

LOCATION OF COURT	WAS PLAN CONFIRMED?	DATE CONFIRMED	WAS PLAN COMPLETED?	CASE NUMBER	NAME OF JUDGE

If you ever filed a Bankruptcy, give the Case Number

_____

Judge's name _____
Location of court _____
Was discharge granted? _____
If so, when: _____

8. a. Is any of your property NOW in the hands of a COURT APPOINTED person (a receiver or trustee)?
      [ ] YES [ ] NO

      Give details on an attached sheet.

    b. Have you made any general assignment of your property for benefit of all your creditors, or any general settlement with all of your creditors during the last TWO years? DO NOT INCLUDE repossessions or payments to individual creditors. [ ] YES [ ] NO

      If YES, attach sheet and explain.

9. Is any person holding anything of value in which you have an interest? [ ] YES [ ] NO   If YES, give:
Name and address, location and description of property and why they are holding the property:

_____

10.

a. Have you been a plaintiff or defendant in a lawsuit of any kind during the past year? [ ] YES [ ] NO

b. Have you received any summons or subpoenas in the last year? [ ] YES [ ] NO

NAME OF PLAINTIFF & DEFENDANT	NAME OF THE COURT	CASE NUMBER	TYPE OF LAWSUIT (COMPLAINT FOR MONEY, ETC.)	RESULT OF LAWSUIT

c. Has any of your property or wages been taken by Court Order (attached, garnisheed or executed upon) in the last FOUR MONTHS? [ ] YES [ ] NO
If YES, list:

PROPERTY OR AMOUNT OF WAGES	NAME OF CREDITOR WHO TOOK THE PROPERTY OR WAGES	DATES TAKEN

11. Have you made any payment to any creditor during the last TWELVE MONTHS? [ ] YES [ ] NO
If YES, list:

_____

_____

TO WHOM PAID NAME & ADDRESS	A RELATIVE?	AMOUNT OF EACH PAYMENT/DATE	FULL AMOUNT OF LOAN	DATE OBTAINED

NOTE: If you only made regular monthly payments and not a lump sum payment, simply write, "MONTHLY PAYMENTS ONLY" and go on to question number 12. Give the date of your last monthly payment.

12.

a & b. Have you sold or given away any property or money during the last SIX YEARS? [ ] YES [ ] NO
If YES, list:

DESCRIPTION OF PROPERTY	NAME & ADDRESS OF PERSON OR COMPANY TO WHOM YOU GAVE OR SOLD PROPERTY	WAS PERSON A RELATIVE?	DATE SOLD OR GIVEN	WHAT WAS RECEIVED BY YOU IN RETURN?

What did you do with the proceeds? _____

DESCRIPTION OF PROPERTY	VALUE OF PROPERTY	CAUSE OF LOSS	DATE OF LOSS	INSURED?

14. Have you consulted any attorney during the prior year other than JACOBY & MEYERS, relative to declaring bankruptcy? [ ] YES [ ] NO

IF YES,   DATE:_____ATTORNEY NAME: _____

AMOUNT PAID:_____DATE PAID: _____

SCHEDULE OF CURRENT INCOME AND EXPENDITURES

A. If unmarried, give your current monthly income. If married, give information for each spouse whether single or joint petitions filed. If spouses are separated, give only your information. This information is required pursuant to Bankruptcy Amendment and Federal Judgeship Act of 1984.

	H, W or J.	$
(1) Debtor's monthly take-home pay	_____	_____
(2) Spouse's monthly take-home pay	_____	_____
(3) Regular income available from operation of a business or profession	_____	_____
(4) Do you receive alimony, maintenance or support payments? If so, state monthly amount	_____	_____

State the name, age and relationship to you of persons for whose benefit payments are received:

_____

(5) Pension, social security or retirement income	_____	_____
(6) Other income (specify)	_____	_____

_____

_____

_____

CURRENT EXPENDITURES

H, W, or J. ___$___

B. Give current monthly expenditures of family consisting of:

(1) Rent or home mortgage payment (include lot rental for trailer) ___ ___

(2) Utilities: (Electricity $___)

(Heat $___)

(Water $___)

(Telephone $___) ___ ___

(3) Food ___ ___

(4) Clothing ___ ___

(5) Laundry & Cleaning ___ ___

(6) Newspapers, periodicals, and books (include school books) ___ ___

(7) Medical & Drug Expense ___ ___

(8) Insurance (not deducted from wage) ___ ___

(Auto: $___)

(Other: $___) ___ ___

(9) Transportation ___ ___

(10) Recreation ___ ___

(11) Dues, union, professional, social or otherwise (not deducted from wages) ___ ___

(12) Taxes (not deducted from wages) _____ _____

(13) Alimony, maintenance or support payments _____ _____

State the name, age and relationship to you of persons for whose benefit payments are made:

(14) Other payments for support of dependents not living at home _____ _____

(15) Expenditures deducted from wages (specify) _____ _____

(16) Other (Specify) _____ _____

When you have completed this form, please call us for an appointment and please bring with you the following items:

(1) This form.

(2) Deeds, mortgages, contracts on your home and mortgage statements.

(3) Any papers relating to past bankruptcies and wage earner's plan (Chapter 13).

(4) Copies of all tax returns for the past TWO YEARS.

(5) All legal papers, (for example: summonses, complaints, notices of attachments and executions, etc.)

(6) Statements and passbooks for savings or checking accounts for the past TWELVE MONTHS.

APPENDIX B

Chapter 13 Bankruptcy Information Form

The Bankruptcy Court requires the information requested by the questions contained in this form. Complete answers are necessary before we can file your bankruptcy papers with the court.

Instructions

1. Answer completely EACH question on EVERY page. Where you are given a choice of YES or NO, check the correct answer in the brackets. If your answer is YES, give the information which is requested. If a question does not apply, write "Not Applicable."

2. PRINT CLEARLY or TYPEWRITE your answers. We MUST be able to read your answers.

3. Where the name and address of a person or company is asked for, give the full name and complete address INCLUDING the zip code. Be sure the address and zip code are correct. For zip code information, phone 212/974-7411. For an address outside of the New York area, dial the area code of the city you want + 555-1212 (the operator can provide you with an area code). The long distance information (Area Code + 555-1212) can provide you with the phone number of the person or company you are seeking, and possibly an address. If long distance information cannot provide you with an address, you can call the number given and ask the person or company their exact address, including zip code.

NOTE: An incorrect or incomplete address may prevent discharge (cancellation) of your debt.

4. If you do not know the exact amount you owe a creditor, fill in an estimate.

5. If you do not understand a question, put a question mark by it, and discuss it with the attorney when you bring back this form.

6. If you need more space to answer a question, write "SEE ATTACHED" when you run out of space on the form, and continue your answer on a separate piece of paper. Write the number of the question on the paper and attach it to this form.

7. This form must be completed in full whether a single or a joint petition is filed. When information is requested for "each" or "either spouse filing a petition," it should be supplied for both when a joint petition is filed.

1. NAME AND ADDRESS

a) Give full name:

Husband

_____
First   Middle   Last

Wife

_____
First   Middle   Last

b) Where does each spouse filing a petition now reside?

Husband

_____
Street   City   State   Zip Code

Wife

_____
Street   City   State   Zip Code

c) Telephone Number:

Husband

_____

Wife _____

    d) What does each spouse filing a petition consider his or her residence, if different from that listed in (b) preceding?

Husband _____
    Street   City   State   Zip Code

Wife _____
    Street   City   State   Zip Code

2.   OCCUPATION AND INCOME

    a) Give present occupation of each spouse filing a petition. (If more than one, list all for each spouse filing a petition.)

Husband _____

Wife _____

    b) What is the name, address and telephone number of present employer (or employers) of each spouse filing a petition? (Include also any identifying badge or card number with employer.)

Husband _____

Wife _____

    c) If either spouse filing a petition has not been employed by present employer for a period of one year, state the name of prior employer(s) and nature of employment during that period.

Husband _____

Wife   _____

    d) Has either spouse filing a petition oper-
    ated a business, in partnership or other-
    wise, during the past three (3) years? (If
    so, give the particulars, including names,
    dates and places.)

Husband   _____

Wife   _____

All information should be given for husband and wife unless spouses are separated and a single petition is filed:

	Husband	Wife
1. Is your current pay period:		
a. Weekly	_____	_____
b. Semi-monthly	_____	_____
c. Monthly	_____	_____
d. Other	_____	_____
Specify _____		
2. What are your gross wages or commission per pay period?	_____	_____
3. What are your payroll deductions per pay period for:		
a. Payroll Taxes (Including Social Security)	_____	_____
b. Insurance	_____	_____
c. Credit Union	_____	_____
d. Union Dues	_____	_____

e. Other   _____ _____

      Specify _____

4. What is your take home pay
per pay period?   _____ _____

5. Is your employment subject to
seasonal or other change?   _____ _____

6. What is the amount of your
gross income for the last cal-
endar year?   _____ _____

7. Has either of you made any wage assignments or alot-
ments? (If so, indicate which spouse's wage was assigned
or alotted, the name and address of the person to whom
assigned or alotted, and the amount owing, if any, to such
person. If alotment or assignment is to a creditor, his claim
should also be listed in Item 11a.)

Husband   _____

Wife   _____

3. DEPENDENTS:
(To be answered for each spouse whether
single or joint petition is filed unless spouses
are separated and a single petition is filed.)

a) Does either of you pay (or receive) alimony, maintenance, or support?

_____

If so, how much per month? _____
For whose support? (Give name, age and
relationship to you.) _____

Answer the following question:
For debtor, if single, or each spouse whether
single or joint petition filed:

Husband   _____

Wife   _____

    b) List all other dependents, other than present spouse, not listed in (a) preceding. (Give name, age and relationship to you.)

Husband   _____

Wife   _____

4.   FUTURE INCOME

    a) Give estimated average future monthly income for each spouse whether single or joint petition is filed *unless* spouses are separated and a single petition is filed.

1.   Husband's Monthly Take-Home Pay $_____

2.   Wife's Monthly Take-Home Pay $_____

3.   Other Monthly Income (Specify) $_____

                                   Total $_____

    b) Give estimated average future monthly expenses of family (not including debts to be paid under plan), consisting of:

1.   Rent or Home Mortgage Payment (Include Lot Rental for Trailer) $_____

2.   Utilities

      Electricity $_____

      Heat $_____

Water $_____

Telephone $_____

3. Food $_____

4. Clothing $_____

5. Laundry and Cleaning $_____

6. Newspaper, Periodicals and Books (Include School Books) $_____

7. Medical and Drug Expense $_____

8. Insurance (Not Deducted from Wages)

Automobile $_____

Other (Specify) $_____

_____

9. Transportation (not including auto payments to be paid under plan)

10. Recreation $_____

11. Club and Union Dues (Not Deducted from Wages) $_____

12. Taxes (Not Deducted from Wages) $_____

13. Alimony, Maintenance of Support Payments $_____

14. Other Payments for Support of Dependents not Living at Home $_____

15.   Other (Specify) $ _____

5.   PAYMENT OF ATTORNEY:

    a) How much have you agreed to pay or what property have you agreed to transfer to Jacoby & Meyers in connection with this case?

    b) How much have you paid or what have you transferred to us?

6.   TAX REFUNDS:

    a) To what tax refunds (income or other), if any, is either of you, or may either of you be, entitled? (Give particulars, including information as to any refunds payable jointly to you or any other person.)

7.   FINANCIAL ACCOUNTS, CDs, SAFE DEPOSIT BOXES:

To be answered for each spouse whether single or joint petition is filed, unless spouses are separated and a single petition is filed.

    a) Does either of you currently have any bank or savings and loan accounts, checking or savings? (If so, give name and address of bank, nature of account, current balance and name and address of every other person authorized to make withdrawals from the account.)

    b) Does either of you currently keep any safe deposit boxes or other depositories? (If so, give name and address of bank or other depository, name and address of every other person who has a right of access thereto, and a brief description of the contents thereof.)

8. PRIOR BANKRUPTCY:

What proceedings under the Bankruptcy Act and Title II, United States Code have previously been brought by or against either spouse filing a petition? (State the location of the bankruptcy court, the nature and number of each proceeding, the date when it was filed and whether a discharge was granted or refused, the proceeding was dismissed or a composition, arrangement, or plan was confirmed.)

9. FORECLOSURES, EXECUTIONS AND ATTACHMENTS:

To be answered for each spouse whether single or joint petition is filed, unless spouses are separated and a single petition is filed.

a) Do you own any real property, including real estate, involved in a foreclosure proceeding, in or out of court? (If so, identify the property and the person foreclosing.)

b) Has any property or income of either of you been attached, garnisheed or seized under any legal or equitable process within the 90 days immediately preceding the filing of the original petition herein? (If so, describe the property seized, or person garnished and at whose suit.)

10. REPOSSESSIONS AND RETURNS:

To be answered for each spouse whether a single or joint petition is filed, unless spouses are separated and a single petition is filed.

      a) Has any property of either of you been returned to, repossessed, or seized by the seller or by any other party, including a landlord, during the 90 days immediately preceding the filing of the original petition herein? (If so, give particulars, including the name and address of the party getting the property and its description and value.)

11.   PRIORITY DEBTS [SCHEDULE A-1]:

      a) and b) If you employed anyone (such as regular employees, cleaning women, gardeners, babysitters) during the last three months, do you still owe him or her wages?
      [ ] YES [ ] NO

If YES, give the name and address of employee, amount owed and dates worked for which you owe the employee wages, and the type of work done. Also, give amounts owed for contributions to employment benefit plan(s) during the last six months.

      c) Have you been given any money as deposit toward the purchase or rental of property, or services for personal, family or household use that you have not provided or delivered? [ ] YES [ ] NO

If YES, give the name and address of person or business who gave the deposit, amount of deposit and property or services for which deposit was made.

      1. Do you owe any taxes to the U.S. Government? [ ] YES [ ] NO

If YES, give the name and address of the department or agency to which the tax is owing, the amount and kind of tax that is owing and the years for which tax is owing.

2. Do you owe any taxes to any state?
[ ] YES [ ] NO

If YES, give the name and address of the department or agency to which the tax is owing, the amount and kind of tax that is owing and the years for which tax is owing.

3. Do you owe any taxes to a county, special district or city? [ ] YES [ ] NO

If YES, give the name and address of the department or agency to which the tax is owing, the amount and kind of tax that is owing and the years for which tax is owing.

11A. DO YOU OWE TAXES TO ANY OTHER TAXING AUTHORITY?

_____

_____

_____

_____

11B. SECURED DEBTS:

List all debts which are or may be secured by real or personal property. (Indicate in sixth column if debt is payable in installments, the amount of each installment, the installment periods [monthly, weekly or other] and number of installments in arrears, if any. Indicate in last column whether husband or wife is solely liable, or whether you are jointly liable.) SEE FOLLOWING CHART.

SECURED DEBTS

NAME AND ADDRESS OF CREDITOR	WHAT DEBT IS FOR	AMOUNT CLAIMED BY CREDITOR	IF DISPUTED, AMOUNT CLAIMED BY YOU	DESCRIPTION OF COLLATERAL*	INSTALLMENT AMOUNT PERIOD & NO. OF INSTALLMENT IN ARREARS	HUSBAND OR WIFE SOLE OR JOINT LIABILITY

*In Description of Collateral, include year and make of automobile.

11C. UNSECURED DEBTS:

List all other debts, liquidated and unliquidated, including taxes, attorneys' fees and tort claims.

CONSIDERATION OR BASIS FOR DEBT	AMOUNT CLAIMED BY CREDITOR	IF DISPUTED, AMOUNT ADMITTED BY DEBTOR	HUSBAND OR WIFE SOLELY OR JOINTLY LIABLE

12. CODEBTORS:

To be answered for each spouse whether single or joint petition is filed.

    a) Are any other persons liable, as cosigners or in any other manner on any of the debts of either of you or are either of you cosigned on the debts of another? (If so, give particulars, indicating which spouse is liable and include names of creditors, nature of debts, names and addresses of codebtors and their relationship, if any, to you.)

    b) If so, have such codebtors made any payments on such debts? (Give name of each codebtor and amount paid by him or her.)

    c) Have either of you made any payments on such debts? (If so, specify total amount paid to each creditor, whether paid by husband or wife, and name of codebtor.)

13. PROPERTY:

To be answered for each spouse whether single or joint petition is filed.

a) REAL PROPERTY:

List all real property owned by either of you at date of filing of original petition herein. (Indicate in last column whether owned solely by husband or wife, or jointly owned.) SEE FOLLOWING CHART.

13A. Do you own your own home, any land, co-op or condominium?   [   ] YES   [   ] NO

If YES, give address and bring in any papers relating to your interest (for example: mortgages, deeds, title insurance, contracts, mortgage statements).

If you own your home, please give:

(1) Date of Purchase _____
(2) Purchase Price _____
(3) Amount of Down Payment _____
(4) Amount Now Owed on First Mortgage _____
(5) Amount Now Owed on Second Mortgage ___
(6) Estimate of the Present Fair Market Value __
(7) The names and relationships to you of anyone whose name is on the deed _____

13B. PERSONAL PROPERTY:

a) How much cash do you have on hand (not in banks)? _____

b) Do you now have any money deposited anywhere (bank checking or savings, savings and loan association, credit un-

REAL PROPERTY

DESCRIPTION AND LOCATION OF PROPERTY	NAME OF ANY CO-OWNER OTHER THAN SPOUSE	PRESENT MARKET VALUE W/O DEDUCTION FOR MORTGAGE OR OTHER SECURITY INTERESTS	AMOUNT OF MORTGAGE OR OTHER SECURITY INTEREST ON THIS PROPERTY	NAME OF MORTGAGOR OR OTHER SECURED CREDITOR	VALUE CLAIMED EXEMPT, IF ANY	OWNED SOLELY BY HUSBAND OR WIFE OR JOINTLY

ion)? [ ] YES [ ] NO If YES, give the following:

NAME AND ADDRESS OF BANK OR INSTITUTION	CHECKING OR SAVINGS	AMOUNT NOW ON DEPOSIT

c) Estimate the value (what you could get if you had to sell quickly) of all your furniture and all your appliances. $_____

Describe any SINGLE item of your furniture or appliances worth more than $200.00.

d) Have you any rare books, prints, paintings or pictures of value? [ ] YES [ ] NO If YES, give the value of all your books $_____ and the value of all your prints, paintings and pictures $_____.

e) Estimate the value (what you could get if you had to sell quickly) of all your clothing $_____; all your jewelry $_____; all your firearms and sports equipment $_____.

f) Do you have any vehicles (autos, tractors, motor bikes, trailers, etc.)? [ ] YES [ ] NO If YES, give:

YEAR	MAKE	MODEL	MARKET VALUE	AMOUNT OWING

g) Do you have any boats, motors or their accessories? [ ] YES [ ] NO
If YES, indicate value $_____
and describe:

_____

h) Do you have any horses, cows, sheep or other animals? (Do not include pets unless valuable.)
[ ] YES [ ] NO If YES, indicate value $_____ and describe:

_____

i) Do you have any crops or farming equipment? [ ] YES [ ] NO If YES, indicate value $_____
and describe:

_____

j) Do you have any office equipment, furnishings, and supplies?
[ ] YES [ ] NO If YES, indicate value $_____ and describe:

_____

k) Do you have any machinery, fixtures, or tools used in your business or occupation (other than those listed in Items j and i)? [ ] YES [ ] NO If YES, indicate value $_____ and describe:

_____

l) Do you have stock in trade (inventory) from any business?
[ ] YES [ ] NO

If YES, indicate value $_____ and describe:

_____

m) Do you have anything of value not listed above that could be considered a piece of property, real or personal?
[ ] YES [ ] NO If YES, indicate value $_____ and describe:

_____

n) Do you have any patents, copyrights, trademarks, or franchises?
[ ] YES [ ] NO
If YES, indicate value $_____ and describe:

_____

o) Do you have any government or other type of bonds? [ ] YES [ ] NO
If YES, indicate value $_____ and describe:

_____

p) Does anyone owe you money?
[ ] YES [ ] NO If YES, indicate his or her name, address and amount he or she owes you:

NAME	ADDRESS	AMOUNT OWED YOU

q) Are you owing, or do you intend to sue anyone, for personal injury or money owed to you or other members of your family? [ ] YES [ ] NO If YES, describe and give amounts you are suing or will sue for:

---

r) Do you have any life insurance policies? [ ] YES [ ] NO If YES, list the following (if you have a small life and health policy through your job or union, simply state "Life and Health Through Employer"):

NAME OF INSURANCE COMPANY	TYPE OF POLICY	ANNUAL PREMIUM	CANCELLATION OR SURRENDER VALUE

---

s) Do you have interest in an annuity? [ ] YES [ ] NO If YES, indicate value $_____ and describe:

---

t) Do you have any stocks or bonds? [ ] YES [ ] NO If YES, indicate value $_____ and describe:

---

u) Do you have any interest in partnership? [ ] YES [ ] NO If YES, indicate value $_____ and describe:

---

      v) Are you a holder of any future power of interest in real property or is any real property being held for you by someone else? Is any real property being held in trust for you? [ ] YES [ ] NO If YES, indicate value $_____ and describe:

When you have completed this form, please call us for an appointment and please bring with you the following items:

1. This form.
2. Deeds, mortgages, contracts on your home and mortgage statements.
3. Any papers relating to past bankruptcies and wage earner's plan (Chapter 13).
4. Copies of tax returns for the past two years.
5. All legal papers (for example: summonses, complaints, notices of attachments and executions, etc.).
6. Statements and passbooks for savings or checking accounts for the past 12 months.

INDEX

Adjustment of individual's debt, 15

Aid to dependent children, 33

Alimony
exemption of income from, 33
nondischargeable debts for, 36, 44

American Bankers Association, 1

Annuities, 33

Anticipated future income, 33

Assets
conversion of, 28–29
detailed list of, 21
exempt, 8–9, 29, 31–35
hidden, 36
liquidation of, 8, 9, 15, 16, 29, 30
seizure of, 8

Bank Account Restraining Notice, 8

Bank accounts, exempt, 32

Bank credit cards. *See* Credit card debt

Bank loans, 14, 28

Bankruptcy laws, 15–17

Bankruptcy Reform Act (1978), 16

Better Business Bureau, 7

Building materials, 33–34

Burial property, 33

Business failures, 17

Car loans, 1, 11
reaffirmation of, 35

Cemeteries, 33

Chapter 7 bankruptcy, 15, 17, 22–25, 28–38, 43, 44

Chapter 11 bankruptcy, 22

Chapter 13 bankruptcy, 15–17, 22–25, 39–45

Checking accounts, 28

Child support obligations, 33, 44

Clothing, exemption from seizure of, 9
Collection agencies, 6–7
Confession of judgment, 12
Congress, U.S., 6, 16
Consolidation loans, 10–11, 14
Constitution, U.S., 15
Conversions of assets, 28–29
Corporate bankruptcy, 19
Cosigners, 35, 40
Court appearances, 22–24
Credit card debt, 1, 2, 14, 18, 28
   minimum monthly payment of, 5
Creditors
   collection agencies hired by, 6–7
   defrauding of, 17
   legal actions taken by, 7–9
   meeting of, 34, 42
   notification of, 34
   reduced-payment plans with, 12
   secured, 35
Crime victim's compensation, 33

Death benefits, exemption from seizure of, 9
Debts, 1, 4
   business, 17
   collection agencies and, 6–7
   consolidation loans, 10–11
   detailed list of, 21
   discharge of, 34–36, 43–44
   imprisonment for, 15
   inability to handle, 3

   legal action on, 7–9
   reduced payment plans, 11–12
   unmanageable, 5, 10, 14, 17
Default, 6, 35, 44
Denial of discharge, 36
Disability benefits, 32
Discharge of debts, 35–36, 43–44
Discharge hearing, 24
Discovery procedures, 8
Dunning letters, 6

English law, 15
Equity, preservation of, 17

Federal Reserve, 1
Filing fees, 29, 41
Fines, 36
Fraud, 28, 29, 36
Future credit, effects on, 36

Garnishment of wages, 3, 9–10, 17, 24, 40

Harassment by collection agencies, 6, 7, 24
Hardship discharges, 44
House, exemption for, 8–9, 32, 33
Household property, exemption for, 9, 32

Information forms, 23, 30–31, 41
Injury, compensation for, 32
Insolvency, 28

Insurance policies, cash value of, 32
Interest rates, 2
   on consolidation loans, 10, 11

Jewelry, exemption for, 32
Job loss, 14
Judgment, 8
   confession of, 12
   garnishment of wages and, 9–10
   seizure of assets and, 8–9

Legal actions by creditors, 7–9
Library materials, 34
Life insurance benefits, 32
Liquidation of assets, 8, 9, 16
   in Chapter 7 bankruptcy, 15, 29, 30
   exemptions from, 8–9, 29, 31–34
Loans
   bank, 14, 28
   consolidation, 10–11
   student, 17, 36
Losses, compensation for, 32

Maintenance payments
   exemption of income from, 33
   as nondischargeable debts, 36
Medical bills, 14
Meeting of creditors, 34
Mortgage payments, 1

Motor vehicles, exemption from seizure of, 32

Penalties, government, 36
Pension plan proceeds, 9, 32, 33
Personal effects, exemption from seizure of, 9, 32
Personal property, exemption from seizure of, 9, 32
Petition, filing of, 29–30, 34, 40–41
Plan of repayment, 41–44
Proceedings supplementary to judgment, 8
Process servers, 8
Professional books, exemption of, 32
Professionals, 40
Profit-sharing plan payments, 32
Public assistance benefits, 32, 33
Purchase agreements, 6

Reaffirmation of debt, 35
Reduced-payment plans, 11–12, 14
Repayment, plan of, 41–44
Residential property exemption. *See* House, exemption for
Retirement benefits, 33
Revocation of discharge, 36
Russell, Barry, 14

Secured debts, 35, 41, 44

Seizure of assets, 8
  exemptions from, 8–9
Small business owners, 40
Social Security benefits, 32
State laws, exemptions under,
  31, 33–34
Student loans, 17
  as nondischargeable debts,
  36
Summonses, 8
Support payments, 33

Taxes due, 35–36, 44
Tax refunds, 32
Tools of your trade, exemption
  of, 9, 32

Trustee in bankruptcy, 24, 29,
  34, 42

Unemployment compensation,
  32
U.S. Bankruptcy Courts, 22
Unsecured debts, 35, 41, 42,
  44

Veteran's benefits, 33

Wage earners, 40
Wages, garnishment of, 3, 9–
  10, 17, 24, 40
Writ of Execution, 8